Magnet Magic

Michael Herschell

Illustrated by
Diana Bowles

4

You could use a magnet!

Magnets have the power to attract some kinds of metal. They stick to steel cans but not to aluminium ones. Try it!

6

My spoon sticks to the magnet like glue but my pencil doesn't.

Magnets don't attract everything. They don't work on plastic, wood or fabrics.

7

Look, there's a long magnet around the fridge door.

My numbers have magnets on the back, too.

One end of a magnet is called the north pole and the other end is called the south pole.

Look, my magnets are pushing each other away!

The north pole of a magnet attracts the south pole of another magnet but it will push another north pole away.

Magnetic power can work through paper, thin wood and glass. It even works through water.

11

If you stroke a steel nail with a magnet for about one minute the nail will turn into a magnet, too. You must always stroke it in the same direction.

The arrow pointer in a compass is magnetic. The earth is magnetic, too. The magnet in the arrow points it to the north pole of the earth. That is how people use compasses to find their way around.

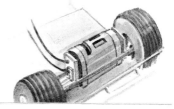

The electric motors that start a car and work the fan need magnets to work. There are magnets in the tape player and magnets in the loudspeakers, too.

Electric cars and trucks cannot work at all without magnets.

I bet the motor in that electric train has a magnet, too.

That's right, it does. But there are some amazing trains that actually float above a magnetic track.

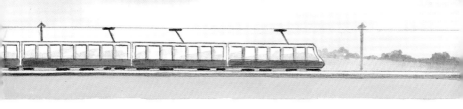

On a Maglev train there are magnets on the train and in the track. The magnets on the track push away the magnets on the train. This makes the train float above the track as it whizzes along.

20

The magnet in the crane works by electricity. When the electricity is switched on the magnet works and the crane picks up the scrap metal.

When the electricity is switched off the magnet stops working and the crane lets the metal go.

21

23

It's an electricity generator. It turns three thousand times a minute. There is a huge magnet inside it. The magnet helps the generator to make enough electricity to light seven million light bulbs.

There is a magnet turning inside the coil of copper wire. This makes electricity.

Now the bulb
has lit up.

29

Here are lots of things that use magnets to make them work. Can you remember them all? The answers are at the bottom of the page.

1

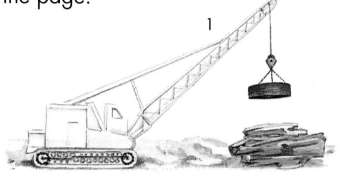

2

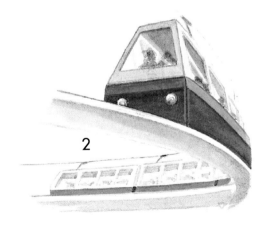